Simply Splendid Smacks

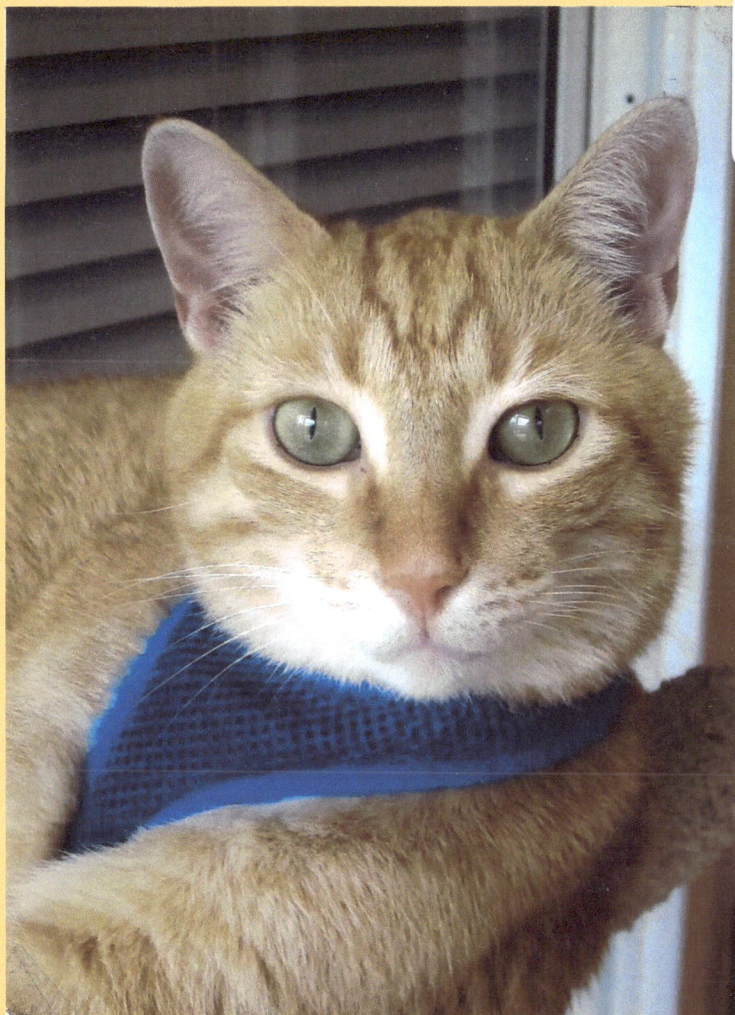

By Jane Fliegner Blythe

ISBN:978-0-692-60448-9

Published by: Grammie & A.B.W. Lexi

Simply Splendid Smacks

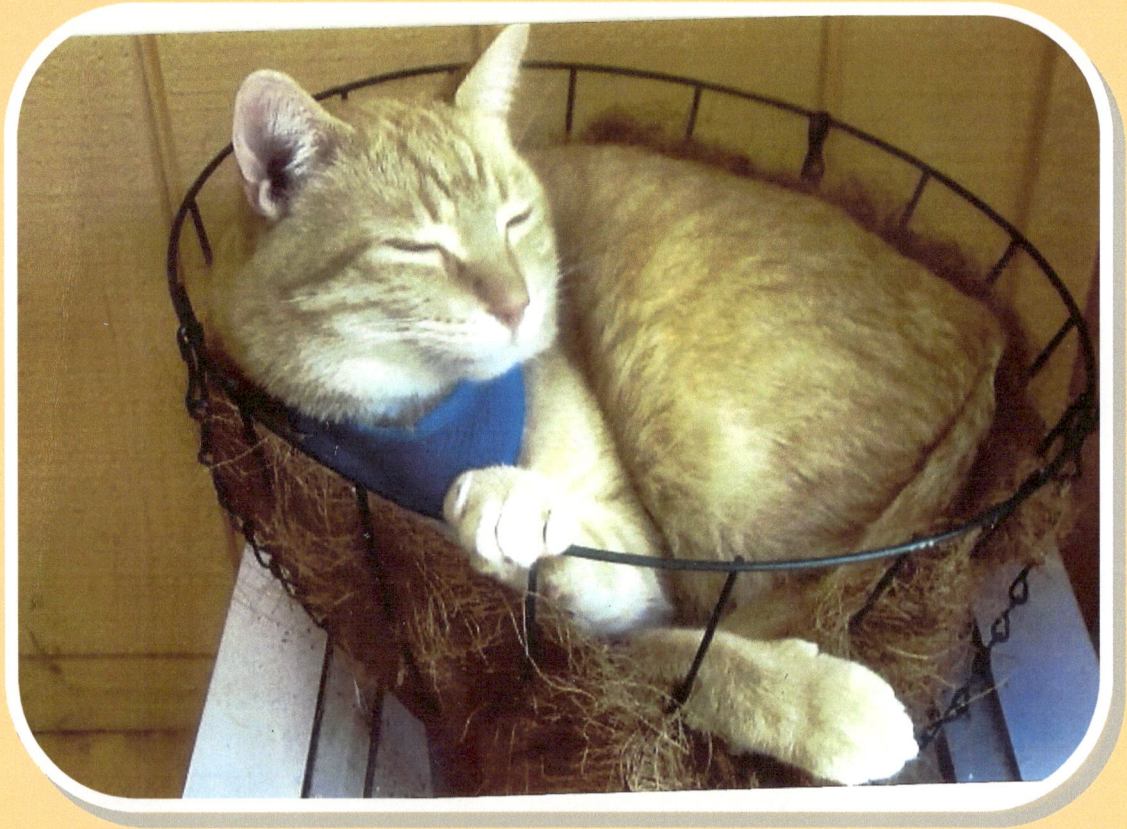

To every cat who has ever been ....to those who own people, to those who are feral, to those who live in animal shelters, to those who are abandoned.....I truly love you all.

To my parents, Carl and Fay Fliegner, who taught me how to care about all sentient beings -- who were loving enough to let me grow up in a kind, happy home filled with dogs, cats, birds, a duck, an injured squirrel....thank you for an incredible legacy.

To Wayne for rescuing our beloved Smacks

and as always, to Alexis.

My name is Smacks, and I am a very special cat, a simply splendid one, if I do say so myself. Of course, each cat has his or her own personality, but everyone who ever sees me out walking in my harness (with a leash) always remarks that they have NEVER seen a cat like me.

I am an Orange Tabby …. and although Orange Tabbies might look ordinary, we are not. As a matter of fact, we tabbies are descendants of the very first cats that came to America!

My human, Jane, drew this picture of me and some of the cats in the shelter.

Here is my very own story....

When I was only six weeks old, the people with whom I had lived— since I was born—brought me to an animal shelter in Lee County, Florida, and JUST LEFT ME THERE!!

They handed me over to people in dark uniforms whom I had never seen before. That was the worst day of my whole life.

It was noisy and quite frightening as they put me in a cage, in a room with two dozen other metal cages. They were filled with many young cats who cried a lot. There were also some older cats and a mother cat with her babies. We were all very, very scared.

3

The folks who worked there tried to be nice to us, giving us fresh water and dry food, but the cages were lonely. I could not understand why my people had left me there.

Can you imagine how confused and alone I felt?? Sometimes a volunteer (someone who helps and does not get paid; does it because they like animals and want to help) would come to take me out of the cage and brush me. However, they always had to put me back in the cage, and at night all of us cats were alone. Sometimes when I drifted off to sleep, a kitten would cry and awaken me. I could not tell the difference between night and day, there were no windows in the room. Many times cats were taken out of their cages by the people in the uniforms and never came back.

Now the good news! I was very fortunate (lucky) because after only a few days, a tall, slender man with glasses and a nice smile came to visit. Out of all-l-l the cats and kittens in the room, he picked me up to play with him. It was a surprise that he saw me, as I was hiding in the back of my cage behind a little blanket that some nice person had placed in the cage with me. It actually had become my security blanket (like small children have).

This man was allowed to take me out of the cage (hurrah!), talk to me and sit with me on his lap. He rubbed me behind my ears, then gently patted my back, all the way down to my tail...I think, perhaps, that was when he noticed what an amazing tail I have, but I'm not 100% sure.

It really is special and I am quite proud of my tail, considering it to be one of my finest features. I wagged my tail straight up in the air and purred, so the man would know how much I enjoyed being with him. I curled up my little front paws and patted them on his chest so he would know how happy I felt (some people call it 'making muffins') Isn't that cute?

6

Well, I started to fall asleep in the tall man's lap because it felt very comfy and warm... then the man talked to an ACO (Animal Control Officer) there and they placed me back in the cage. That was terribly sad and confusing for me. I was so upset that I hid in the corner of the cage behind my blanket. I could not eat or drink...

What I did not know was that he (Wayne) would be back soon with his wife (Jane) as he wanted to be positive she liked me, too. What I also did not know was that he had told the ACO that he was sure she would love me. He planned to take me home with him in a few days, so they placed a sign on my cage saying "Adopted"!

Adopted—what a special, wonderful word!

A couple of days later—on Valentines' Day—Mr. Wayne and Mrs. Jane came to the shelter, paid for me and signed some papers, then hugged and kissed me while they carried me to their car. Jane kept whispering in my ear how much she loved me and talked to me all the way to my new home.

They had a nice cat carrier in the car in case I became nervous or restless because of all the changes in my life. But I was so content (happy, calm) that it was natural and easy to snuggle in her arms and just fall asleep. Now I was going to my forever home and there were a lot of adventures to come, for a six week old tabby kitten.

I like my afternoon nap

When we reached home, my people showed me right away where their bathroom was—because my litter box was there, too. Cats are very smart, and as an especially intelligent cat, I knew right away how to use the litter box.

Then they showed me my new toys and my climbing tree—I call it a climbing tree, or my "kitty condo", but it was pieces of wood covered with carpeting; it had different sections to sleep on, as well as a large rough area on which I would sharpen my claws.

I still had claws because many people believe it is painful and harmful to declaw cats! I learned to use my scratching post right away and did not harm the furniture at all.

Wayne and Jane then walked me around our new house a few times, so I could become accustomed to my new environment (surroundings, places around me).... there were SO many windows to look out, and big glass doors where I could see the trees and all the birds flying around— this was quite exciting!!

Then my people showed me where they kept my food... there was a big tray on the kitchen floor with a bowl of cold water, a bowl of dry food (which tasted really yummy), as well as a small dish of moist food. It tasted way better than the food they provided at the animal shelter.

My people let me walk around the house, smell things and investigate by myself in order to help me feel comfortable in my new home.

Suddenly I remember feeling really tired…. all the excitement had made me feel very sleepy. Jane placed me in a soft round bed near her chair and patted me on the head until I fell asleep. She and Wayne were sitting near me with the television on, and I slept for quite awhile. When I finally did awaken, Wayne picked me up and brushed me. I climbed onto his right shoulder and cuddled against his neck—it felt so warm and nice, just as if I had always been there.

It was nice to watch the television for a while with them, and I could even see some colors (people do not realize just how bright we cats are).

How wonderful to belong and to have such a nice family. They loved me as much as I loved them ......and still do.

14

Before too long, I jumped off Wayne's shoulder, walked into my new kitchen and had something to eat—this was going to be great!!

Obviously my new people are animal oriented, and knew something that many folks do not realize—more people in the United States own cats than dogs (ha, ha to you canines). Of the folks who do own cats, more than 50% have more than one cat (so in the future I may get a brother or sister cat). However, only about 20% of cats who are owned come from animal shelters.

I am very fortunate to have been adopted and hope that people who meet me will be impressed and decide that they too would like to find a cat and give him or her a 'forever home'.

EXCEPT for three things that happened next....
the accident, my operation and my travels
(to be continued).

15

Many people feel that we tabbies are very intelligent and get along extremely well with people. My human companions definitely agree and also feel that I am a lot like a dog.

When a gardener is working near our house, I hiss to alert Jane that there is potential danger.

When I was six weeks old, Jane tried placing a harness on me—it didn't bother me at all and as I grew she bought a larger harness for me. Now when I want to go outside, I sit in front of the door and meow: when my human starts to put my harness on me, I stand quietly and step into it. After she attaches the leash, I pull forward and walk all over the yard and the neighborhood—-especially enjoyable are long walks on the grass, peeking into the bushes and investigating all the different smells.

Walking into the bushes, trying to see all the little lizards, my gorgeous tail protrudes, everyone who walks by ask Jane, " What kind of dog is that?" It is SO FUNNY! People think only dogs walk on leashes.

17

Do you want to adopt a cat???

Please look in a shelter! Maybe if you know more about us cats you may want to have one of us (or two of us) live with you…..

Here are some facts that you might not know about how special we cats are… we actually can smell better than human beings, have better eyesight at night, and also have much better hearing that dogs and humans too. My, we really are interesting little creatures, aren't we?

Some cats hear their owners coming home and greet them at the door the way a dog does! Oh, and we can make over 100 sounds. Also people can learn a lot about how we cats feel by looking at our tails — yes, that is true! If our tails are straight up and a little curved at the tip, it means that we are happy. If our tails are straight up and shaking it means that we are feeling friendly. However, if my tail is being held straight up, but the tip of it is twitching back and forth quickly, you might want to leave me alone for awhile as I may be grumpy. This doesn't happen very often, but we felines (cats) need our 'alone' time just like humans do.

Don't I look cute in my Christmas tie? I love to dress up for the Holidays.

Before Christmas I wore my decorated collar and tie. When Jane rang the bell for the Salvation Army Bucket Campaign, I went with her, sat on my carrier and greeted guests outside the store. What fun we had!

19

I'm a perfectly handsome Tabby Cat

The term Tabby cat refers to the color and the markings on us. Tabbies can be black, brown or gray. We can have stripes, dots or splotches. Because of my orange color and my markings (mostly stripes), I closely resemble the African Wild Cat.

Also, if you look at all the various colors and designs on tabbies, you still will see an M design on our foreheads... this is typical of a tabby. There are different ideas as to why we have this M design. Why don't you research it and see what YOU think could be the real reason?

I'm a very happy Tabby

Here I am with my British shorthaired friend

Some of my 'fave' things to do

I like to visit my friends

Sleep on Wayne's motorcycle

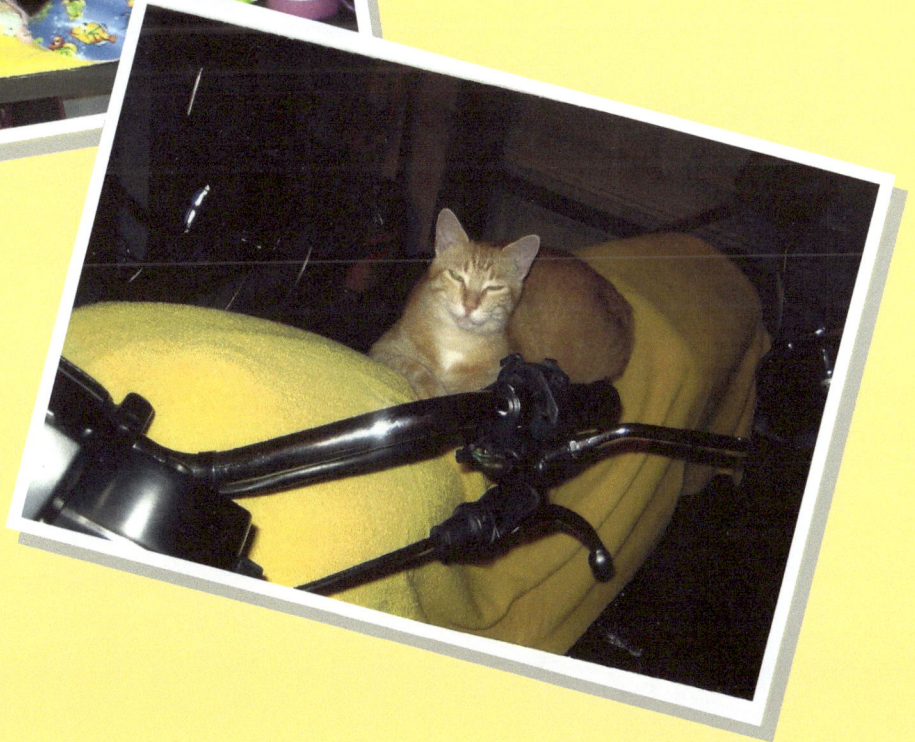

Sometimes I wear caps on
my nails so I can't
scratch the furniture

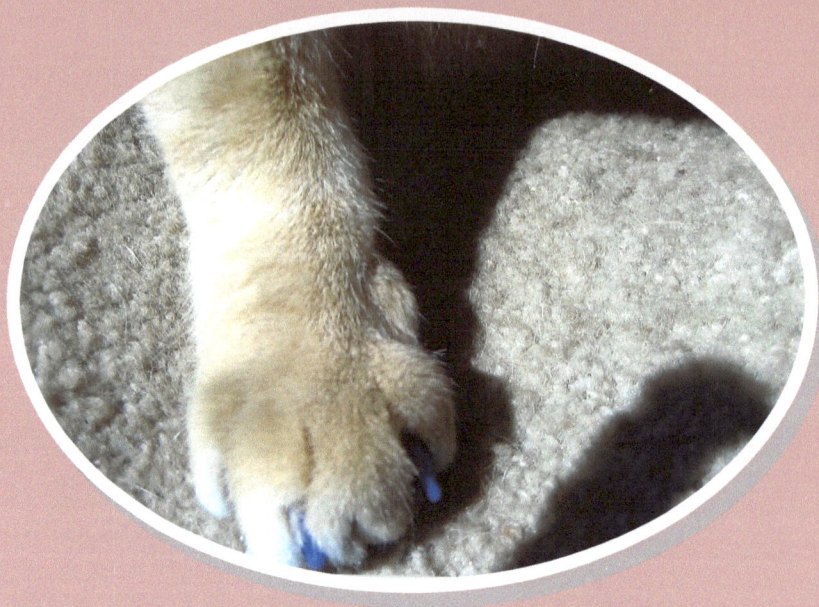

If I want a good scratch,
my scratch toy is the best.

Sometimes I help with the laundry.

Always stretch before exercising.

It's always more fun to exercise with a friend.

My very favorite thing is getting a good hug. Not too tight now! Especially when Lexi, my human's granddaughter, visits. She gives the best cuddles ever.

I am also a very patriotic cat

I dress up every Fourth of July

God Bless America

Bye for now.... I hope you enjoyed
my story.

Other books by this author

My Grandmother's Backyard Wildlife Sanctuary

"Legend" - The Mascot of Parris Island

Coming soon

"Do Turtles have Teeth?"